D1491435

0000180388973

Pulleys

BY KATIE MARSICO • ILLUSTRATED BY REGINALD BUTLER

The Child's World®

Published by The Child's World®
1980 Lookout Drive • Mankato, MN 56003-1705
800-599-READ • www.childsworld.com

Acknowledgments
The Child's World®: Mary Berendes, Publishing Director
The Design Lab: Cover and interior design
Amnet: Cover and interior production
Red Line Editorial: Editorial direction

Photo credits
Matt Harris/iStockphoto, cover, 1; José Pedro Coelho/
iStockphoto, 7; Derek R. Audette/Shutterstock Images, 9;
Robert J. Beyers II/Shutterstock Images, 12; Dmitry
Kalinovsky/Shutterstock Images, 14; Repina Valeriya/
Shutterstock Images, 19; iStockphoto, 23

Design elements: In.light/Dreamstime

Copyright © 2013 by The Child's World®
All rights reserved. No part of this book may be
reproduced or utilized in any form or by any means
without written permission from the publisher.

ISBN 9781614732754
LCCN 2012933654

Printed in the United States of America
Mankato, MN
July 2012
PA02120

ABOUT THE AUTHOR

Katie Marsico is the author of more than 100 children's and young-adult reference books. She uses a pulley to dry her clothes on the clothesline in spring.

ABOUT THE ILLUSTRATOR

Reginald Butler is a professional artist whose work includes poetry, painting, design, animation, commercial graphics, and music. One day he hopes to wake up and read his comic in the paper while watching his cartoon on television.

Table of Contents

Tools and Machines

What would your life be like without tools and machines? You use tools and machines every day. Tools and machines help you do **work**. Computers are machines that help you store information. Cars are machines that help you move from place to place. Washing machines help you clean your clothes. These kinds of machines have many moving parts. Machines with many moving parts are **complex**. Complex machines are made up of many simple machines. There are six types of simple machines. They are pulleys, inclined planes, wedges, screws, levers, and wheels. It's time to find out about pulleys. Get ready to learn how a little pull can go a long way!

Pulleys help you play and work outside.

Lift and Lower

A pulley is a type of wheel that has raised edges. The wheel has a **groove** in the middle. A rope or cable runs in the groove. Either the rope or the wheel is attached to an object that needs to be moved. Pulleys help you lift and lower loads that might be too heavy to move on your own. Pulleys also help you raise or lower an object by changing the direction of a force.

Ropes can go in between the grooves of a pulley.

Raise It Up

There are two types of pulleys. Fixed pulleys are the first type. A fixed pulley is attached to a surface that sits above or on the side of the load that is moved. The wheel on this pulley turns. But the whole pulley does not move. Flagpoles, window blinds, and clotheslines use fixed pulleys.

A fixed pulley is connected to
a wall, or another
fixed surface.

A well has a pulley for raising a
bucket of water.

Fixed pulleys change the direction of force you create when you pull on the rope. You pull down on the rope. But the object on the other end of the rope is raised. A fixed pulley makes it easier to lift something above your head.

GETTING WATER

A well uses a fixed pulley. Letting the rope out lets the bucket dip into the water. Pulling on the other end brings the bucket back up.

Have you ever raised a flag on a flagpole? You probably used a pulley! The wheel sits at the top of the pole. A rope runs between the grooves and is attached to the flag. You raise the flag when you pull down on the rope. It would be much harder to climb a ladder and pull the flag up to the top of the pole!

This man uses a pulley to raise the flag.

Movable Pulley

A crane uses a movable pulley to lift its load.

Lifted with the Load

Movable pulleys are another kind of pulley. The wheel is attached to the load being lifted or lowered. This means the pulley is moved along with the object. Movable pulleys add to the distance an object needs to move. But, they decrease the **effort** you need to raise or lower the object. Cranes use movable pulleys at construction sites.

Experimenting with a movable pulley will help you see how the pulley works up close.

Movable pulleys are good if you want to lift a heavy load that is beneath you up to your level. Imagine you are a worker who is helping build a house. You need to raise glass, wood, and metal to the second floor. Would it be easier to move these materials with a pulley or to lift them straight up with a rope?

More Than One Machine

Sometimes people use a movable pulley and a fixed pulley together. This is called a **compound** pulley or a pulley system. You might find a compound pulley in a garage. Take a peek at the ceiling the next time you are in one.

ELEVATOR RIDE

Have you heard of a block and tackle? This is a pulley system usually made up of cable and one or more pulleys that are attached to blocks. A block and tackle with enough pulleys can lift several thousand pounds! Elevators use these pulley systems.

Sailboats use pulley systems to raise and lower the sails.

A man uses a compound pulley to raise his bike to the ceiling.

Some people hang their bikes from their garage ceilings. Yet how do they get the bikes up there?

A person could use a compound pulley to move the bike. Three fixed pulleys attached to the ceiling help lift the bike. Two movable pulleys attached to the bike cut down on the effort needed to lift it.

Pulleys Everywhere

Now you know about pulleys. These simple machines are everywhere! They are in your garage and at construction sites. Pulleys help you hang clothes and keep flags flying high. They make it easier to lift and lower many different objects. How will you use pulleys today?

Some clotheslines use pulleys, too.

GLOSSARY

complex (kuhm-PLEKS): If something is complex, it has a lot of parts. A computer is a complex machine.

compound (KAHM-pound): If something is compound, it is made of two different parts. A compound pulley is made of movable and fixed pulleys.

effort (EF-urt): Effort is the amount of force that must be used to do work. It takes less effort to lift something with a pulley than to lift it without a pulley.

groove (GROOV): A groove is a long, narrow cut in something. A wheel on a pulley has a groove in it.

work (WURK): Work is applying a force, such as pulling or pushing, to move an object. Pulleys help you do work.

BOOKS

Arnold, Nick. *How Machines Work: The Interactive Guide to Simple Machines and Mechanisms.* Philadelphia, PA: Running Press, 2011.

Bodden, Valerie. *Pulleys.* Mankato, MN: Creative Education, 2011.

Gosman, Gillian. *Pulleys in Action.* New York: PowerKids Press, 2011.

WEB SITES

Visit our Web site for links about pulleys:
childsworld.com/links

Note to Parents, Teachers, and Librarians: We routinely verify our Web links to make sure they are safe and active sites. So encourage your readers to check them out!

INDEX